What Is the
FOREVER
FOREIGNER
STEREOTYPE?

VIRGINIA LOH-HAGAN

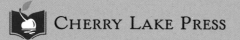

Published in the United States of America by Cherry Lake Publishing Group
Ann Arbor, Michigan
www.cherrylakepublishing.com

Reading Adviser: Beth Walker Gambro, MS, Ed., Reading Consultant, Yorkville, IL
Book Design and Cover Art: Felicia Macheske

Photo Credits: © Africa Studio/Shutterstock.com, 5; © Alena Ozerova/Shutterstock.com, 7; © logoboom/Shutterstock.com, 9; © IKO-studio/Shutterstock.com, 11; © bmf-foto.de/Shutterstock.com, 12; © Sinan Niyazi KUTSAL/Shutterstock.com, 15; © bgrocker/Shutterstock.com, 16; © Dragon Images/Shutterstock.com, 19; © WorldTraveler_1/Shutterstock.com, 21; © mentatdgt/Shutterstock.com, 22; © Pixel-Shot/Shutterstock.com, 25; © Billion Photos/Shutterstock.com, 27; © Dean Drobot/Shutterstock.com, 29; © Phovoir/Shutterstock.com, 30

Graphics Throughout: © debra hughes/Shutterstock.com

Cherry Lake Press is an imprint of Cherry Lake Publishing Group.

Library of Congress Cataloging-in-Publication Data has been filed and is available at catalog.loc.gov.

Cherry Lake Publishing Group would like to acknowledge the work of the Partnership for 21st Century Learning, a Network of Battelle for Kids. Please visit *http://www.battelleforkids.org/networks/p21* for more information.

Printed in the United States of America

Dr. Virginia Loh-Hagan is an author, former K-8 teacher, curriculum designer, and university professor. She's currently the director of the Asian Pacific Islander Desi American (APIDA) Center at San Diego State University. She identifies as Chinese American and is committed to amplifying APIDA communities. She lives in San Diego with her one very tall husband and two very naughty dogs.

CHAPTER 1

What Is the Forever Foreigner Stereotype?

Asian Americans are a strong community. But like other people of color, they are suffering. They are denied justice. They struggle under White **supremacy**.

In the 1960s, activists first used the term "Asian American." They sought to unite Asian groups. Before that, Asian immigrants were known by their ethnicities. For example, they were called "Chinese American" or "Indian American." They acted as separate groups. But they were mistreated as one big group. So they joined forces. As "Asian Americans," they had more power.

Today, they are also called "Asian American Pacific Islander (AAPI)." Another term is "Asian Pacific Islander **Desi** American (APIDA)." These terms are more **inclusive**, meaning that they apply to more Asian people. But they don't fully represent this community. Asian Americans are diverse. They have unique cultures, histories, and languages. It's important to remember this.

Asian Americans are part of the American story. They have made significant contributions and continue to do so. Yet, they are often pushed to the margins. In the 1800s, they immigrated in large numbers. Since then, they have faced **discrimination**. They have fought to be seen and heard. Their fight for racial justice continues today.

Think about what you have learned in school. How many Asian Americans did you study?

Asian Americans fight to be seen as Americans. But they are often seen as perpetual or forever foreigners. They are seen as "the other." The Forever Foreigner stereotype is one of the main causes of anti-Asian hate. A stereotype is a widely held belief about a group of people. It sends the following message: "You are not the same as us. You don't belong here." It's rooted in xenophobia. Xenophobia is the fear or dislike of people from other countries.

The United States has a history of exploiting Asian Americans. Asian workers came in the 1800s. They helped build the Transcontinental Railroad. They worked on farms and opened businesses. They made great contributions. They helped build the country. Many even lost their lives. But they were mistreated. They were supposed to work and then go back to Asia. But many of these workers wanted to stay in the United States. The U.S. government created racist laws to keep Asians out. The Page Act of 1875 banned Chinese women from immigrating. The Chinese Exclusion Act of 1882 banned Chinese workers from immigrating. The Geary Act of 1892 extended these bans. These laws created hate and tension.

This book unpacks the Forever Foreigner stereotype. Learn more so that you can do more. Help fight against White supremacy.

Think about your travels. Have you traveled to a foreign country? How were you treated?

AMPLIFY AN ACTIVIST!

Activists change our world for the better. Stephanie Hu founded "Dear Asian Youth." This is a youth-led platform. It shares stories, resources, and more. She celebrates being Asian. She said, "I felt pressured to act as White as possible.... Looking back, it pains me to see how poorly I treated myself and my heritage."

CHAPTER 2

What Is the History of the Forever Foreigner Stereotype?

Asian Americans first came to the United States in 1587. Sailors from the Philippines landed in Morro Bay, California. In 1763, Filipino fishermen settled in Saint Malo, Louisiana. In the 1800s, more Asian immigrants followed. Today, Asian Americans are the fastest growing ethnic group. Their numbers are expected to triple by 2060. Yet they are often still seen as foreigners.

Amanda Nguyen is an activist. She said, "When you have this perpetual foreigner stereotype, it's easy to scapegoat. The consequence of that has been lives lost." The Forever Foreigner stereotype allows Asian Americans to be blamed for things that aren't their fault.

For example, Asian Americans have been blamed for economic insecurity. During the 1850s, there was much anti-Chinese hate. The Chinese were blamed for White workers losing jobs. Chinese workers were attacked. Some were killed. There were movements against them. The slogan was "The Chinese Must Go!"

In 1982, Vincent Chin was killed. Chin was a Chinese American man living in Detroit, Michigan. Two White men who had lost their jobs at a Detroit car factory killed Chin in a bar. One of them was heard saying, "It's because of you … that we're out of work." At that time, Japanese car companies were popular. They pushed American car companies out of business. Asian Americans were blamed for this.

Think about your family history. How long has your family been in the United States?

Asian Americans have been blamed for national insecurity. Japanese incarceration is the best example of this. In 1941, Japan attacked Pearl Harbor in Hawaii. This caused the United States to enter World War II (1939–1945). President Franklin D. Roosevelt wanted to protect the nation. He signed an order forcing Japanese Americans into camps. These camps were like jail.

More than 120,000 Japanese Americans were kicked out of their homes. They were held in these camps for years. They were not seen as citizens, even though many were born in the United States. They were seen as foreigners. They were seen as the enemy. They had a hard time proving their loyalty. Some joined the U.S. Army 442nd Infantry Regiment. This unit was made up of Japanese American soldiers. They were the most highly decorated U.S. unit in history. But they were still incarcerated.

On September 11, 2001, terrorists attacked the United States. South Asian Americans became "the other." They shared similar looks to the terrorists. Some shared a similar religion. They were blamed for the attacks. Haru Kondabolu is an Indian American comedian. He said South Asians were "victimized twice." First, as

Americans, they were hurt by the terrorist attacks. Second, they were blamed by their fellow Americans.

Think about a bad thing that happened. Did you blame yourself or another person?

LEARN FROM OUR PAST!

Let's not repeat the mistakes of our past. Bhagat Singh Thind emigrated from India. He fought to become a citizen. In 1923, the U.S. Supreme Court denied him. It said he didn't meet the "common sense" definition of White. It said he was foreign. We need to change laws that uphold White supremacy.

Think about the last time you were sick. How did you get sick?

Asian Americans have also been blamed for public health crises. When outbreaks happen, people are scared of becoming sick or dying. This causes fear. In some cases, people panic.

In 1900, **bubonic plague** broke out in San Francisco. Bubonic plague was a deadly disease at the time. Trade ships sailed between Hawaii and San Francisco. Rats carrying the plague landed. Chinese workers were forced to live in Chinatown. They were excluded from other parts of the city. Chinatown was poor and cramped. It was the perfect breeding ground for the plague. A Chinese American man was the first to die of the plague. Officials **quarantined** Chinatown. Chinese Americans were not allowed to leave the area. But White Americans could come and go. This quarantine was motivated more by racism than science. The mayor said Chinese Americans were unclean and "a constant menace to the public health." Chinese American leaders were upset. They fought back. They hired lawyers. The court ruled in favor of the Chinese Americans. It said that restrictions had to apply to all and not just one group. Also, there wasn't enough proof that the Chinese were spreading the plague.

CHAPTER 3

What Does the Forever Foreigner Stereotype Look Like Today?

In December 2019, the COVID-19 pandemic broke out. A pandemic is a disease that spreads through the world. The first case was in China. Then it spread worldwide. The pandemic set the stage for race-based hate based on the Forever Foreigner stereotype.

The World Health Organization (WHO) encourages scientists and leaders to be careful with disease names. It doesn't name diseases after areas or people. It names diseases after science concepts. This helps reduce stigmas, or marks of shame. But President Donald Trump didn't follow the WHO's advice. He called COVID-19 the "Kung Flu" and the "China Virus." Such comments are xenophobic.

Trump's words did a lot of damage. In the United States, anti-Asian violence increased. People blamed the virus on anyone with an Asian background. Asian Americans became victims of hate. They were called racist names. They were harassed in the streets. They were attacked. Many elderly Asian Americans were pushed or beat up. On March 16, 2021, a man began shooting in a spa in Atlanta, Georgia. He killed 6 Asian American women. Bee Nguyen is a Georgia State Representative. She said, "No matter how you want to spin it, the facts remain the same. This was an attack on the Asian community."

Think about what you did during the COVID-19 pandemic. What were some of your fears?

Think about what "Stop Asian Hate" means. How have you helped this cause?

STAY ACTIVE ON SOCIAL!

Stay connected on social media. It is a great way to learn more. Follow these hashtags:

- **#IAmAmerican** This hashtag was launched to highlight World War II Japanese American soldiers. It encourages people of color to share their stories.

- **#WashTheHate** This hashtag was started by Asian American celebrities. It focuses on combating anti-Asian hate.

President Joe Biden said, "Too many Asian Americans have been waking up each morning this past year fearing for their safety and the safety of their loved ones." Asian Americans are more scared of anti-Asian hate than of COVID-19. They can protect themselves against the disease. But they can't protect themselves against hate. Attacks could happen at any time. They could happen anywhere.

Asian American activists fought back. They hosted community safety watches. They organized to protect the elderly. They marched in rallies. They chanted, "We are not a virus." They also chanted, "Asian is not a virus. Racism is." They fought against xenophobia. Being Asian is not the cause of diseases.

Kamala Harris is the vice president of the United States. She is Black and Indian American. She said, "Racism is real in America. And it has always been. Xenophobia is real in America and always has been. Sexism too. The president and I will not be silent. We will not stand by. We will always speak out against violence, hate crimes, and discrimination, wherever and whenever it occurs."

Racism has made it harder for Asian Americans to earn a living. Businesses owned by Asian Americans have suffered. Chinatown communities have collapsed. Kevin Chan is from San Francisco's Chinatown. He owns the Golden Gate Fortune Cookie Factory. He has seen 70 to 80 percent fewer customers. He said, "... Everybody's just scared—scared to come to the Chinese communities." Xenophobia has kept customers away. People think these places are hotspots for the disease. This is far from true. Research shows that there are fewer COVID-19 cases in Chinatowns than other neighborhoods. People cannot catch a disease from an ethnicity. Risk factors aren't connected to race or culture. Risk is connected to behaviors.

Southeast Asians have also been affected. After the Vietnam War (1959–1975), many came to the United States. Since 2020, raids against them have increased. The U.S. Immigration and Customs Enforcement (ICE) has deported many Cambodians. They took them to detention centers. These centers are like jails. Southeast Asians were forced to stay in cramped spaces. They faced an increased risk for COVID-19. They came legally as refugees, which means they fled war and poverty in their home country. Yet, they are still treated like foreigners.

Asian Americans have suffered greatly under COVID-19. It is important to stop the spread of the disease. But it is also important to stop the racial hatred it has created.

Think about an Asian-owned business close to you. How can you support it?

CHAPTER 4

Why Is the Forever Foreigner Stereotype Problematic?

Scapegoating is one of the main problems of the Forever Foreigner stereotype. People fear the unknown. This fear makes people look for scapegoats. Blaming others makes people feel better. It releases them from taking responsibility. It lets them feel more in control. If you identify a villain, then you can be a hero. It's easy to blame foreigners. Foreigners are "not like us."

"Where are you from?" This question is loaded. If Asian Americans answer with a city in the United States, they're asked, "Where are you really from?" When people ask this question, they are usually asking about ethnic backgrounds. Would a White American get asked this question as much? This question assumes people are not from the United States. It assumes they are from another country.

Asian Americans are also often told, "Go back to China." There are several issues with this, First, it assumes all Asian Americans are Chinese. Second, it assumes that the United States is not their country. Third, it fails to recognize that the United States is a country of immigrants. The only people who are truly from here are Native Americans.

Think about where you come from. What does that question mean for you?

Think about the importance of being bilingual. Can you speak another language?

Another common comment is "Your English is really good." It expresses surprise. It assumes Asian Americans do not speak English. It also assumes Asian Americans have accents. More than 4 out of 5 immigrants speak English well. Only four percent of Asian immigrants do not speak any English at all. It is important to note that the United States does not have an official language. English is commonly used, but it shouldn't be treated as the supreme language. People shouldn't be shamed for speaking their heritage languages.

The Forever Foreigner stereotype depicts Asian Americans as outsiders. It doesn't matter where they were born. It doesn't matter how long they have lived in the United States. Asian Americans are not seen as "real Americans." This thinking is racist. It is also incorrect. Asian Americans are not foreigners, guests, or visitors. Today, one-third of Asian Americans were born in the United States. Nearly 50 percent of foreign-born Asian Americans have lived in the United States for more than 20 years. Many Asian American families have been here for several generations.

The Forever Foreigner stereotype has a narrow definition of an "American." Americans are White and are tall. They have light hair and blue eyes. These images are seen over and over again. They are shown in TV, movies, and magazines.

Asian Americans do not fit this definition. As such, some Asian Americans actively work to not look or act Asian. They deny their culture. They stop speaking their language. They even change their looks. They may dye their hair. They may get eyelid surgery. Fred Korematsu fought against Japanese incarceration. He got a lawyer and went to court. He also changed the shape of his eyes. He wanted to look less Asian to avoid racism.

Asian American women are valued for their beauty. But their beauty is seen as exotic. They are seen as special or different. This type of thinking has led to violence against women. It's another example of foreigner stereotyping.

Think about who is featured on TV shows. Why aren't there more Asian Americans?

BE IN THE KNOW!

Other concepts to know:

- **Assimilationism** Non-White groups are seen as inferior. They need to be taught how to be "good Americans." In doing so, they lose their culture.

- **Internalized Racism** Some Asian Americans believe they're foreigners. They rank themselves lower than White people. They disconnect from or reject their heritage cultures.

CHAPTER 5

How Can We Be Better?

Now you have learned about the problems with the Forever Foreigner stereotype. Let's work to abolish it. Let's stop it forever.

We all come from different positions of privilege. We also have different types of privilege. Privilege is a special right or advantage. It is given to a chosen person or group. It isn't earned. In the United States, being White is a privilege. Other examples include being male or an English speaker. It's hard to get ahead in a world that is not made for you. Use your privileges. Help oppressed people achieve equality.

Start with Yourself!

Everybody can do something. Just start somewhere. Start small. Build your self-awareness and your knowledge.

- Learn more about Asian American history. Focus on immigration patterns. Study how and when Asian groups came. Learn about the anti-Asian hate they experienced.

- Learn the difference between Asian and Asian American. Know that Asian Americans have a unique history in this country.

- Learn how to say names correctly. Ask people what they want to be called. Take time to practice names. Respect people's cultures and identities.

- Unlearn American standards of beauty. Expand what it means to be beautiful. Learn from the "Black Is Beautiful" movement. Know that Asian is beautiful.

Think about your privileges. What powers and resources do you have?

Be an Ally!

Being an ally is the first step in racial justice work. Allies recognize their privilege. They use it in solidarity with others. They see something and they say something.

- Speak up when you hear people making fun of another culture. A common example is comments about "weird" food. Don't let people make fun of cultural foods. Have an open mind. Try new foods yourself.

- Speak up if you hear someone saying, "Speak English." Remind them all languages have equal value.

- Speak up if people state wrong information. For example, someone might say, "You can get COVID from eating Chinese food." Correct them. Refer them to resources to learn more.

- Speak up when people say or do offensive things. Report these incidents to Stop AAPI Hate: https://stopaapihate.org/reportincident

Be an Accomplice!

Being an **accomplice** goes beyond allyship. Accomplices use their privilege to challenge supremacy. They are willing to be uncomfortable. They stand up for equal rights.

- Stand united against anti-Asian hate. Participate in peaceful protests. Be safe.

- Stand near a person getting harassed. Record what is happening on your phone. Make sure you are safe. Make sure an adult is with you.

Think about your powers and resources. How would your life be different without them?

Be an Activist!

Activists actively fight for political or social change. They give up their own privileges. They work together to fight against racism. They understand that if one group suffers, all groups suffer.

- Fight for more representation. Seeing Asian Americans in media makes them seem less foreign. Write letters to film and TV companies.

- Fight for voting rights. Help Asian Americans register to vote. Help get Asian Americans elected.

- Fight for Black Lives Matter. Racism in the United States is more than just Black versus White. It is about insiders versus outsiders. Don't let anyone be treated like an outsider.

Think about what you have and what others do not. Do you want to improve the lives of others? What are you willing to give up to do this?

Take the Challenge!

Read all the books in the "Racial Justice in America" series. Engage in the community of activism. Create a podcast, newsletter, video, or social media campaign. Show up for the Asian American community. Include a segment about the Forever Foreigner stereotype.

TASK: Interview several Asian Americans. Include voices from different Asian and Pacific Islander backgrounds. Show how there are different "American" stories. Show how Asian American stories matter. Show how Asian American stories are American stories.

Share your learning. Encourage others to learn more. Then, when you know more, do more. Commit to racial justice!

WHAT WOULD YOU DO?

Imagine you are with your friends. A stranger says to your Vietnamese American friend, "Ching Chong Chong." How does this promote the Forever Foreigner stereotype? What would you do?

☐ Laugh it off.   ☐ Check on your friend.

☐ Pretend it didn't happen.   ☐ Say something.

EXTEND YOUR LEARNING

FICTION

Bajaj, Varsha. *Count Me In*. New York, NY: Puffin Books, 2020.

Kelkar, Supriya. *American as Paneer Pie*. New York, NY: Simon Pulse, 2020.

Yang, Gene Luen. *American Born Chinese*. New York, NY: First Second, 2006.

NONFICTION

Ha, Robin. *Almost American Girl: An Illustrated Memoir*. New York, NY: Balzer + Bray, 2021.

Loh-Hagan, Virginia. *A is for Asian American: An Asian Pacific Islander Desi American Alphabet Book*. Ann Arbor, MI: Sleeping Bear Press, 2022.

Public Broadcasting Service: Asian Americans
www.pbs.org/weta/asian-americans/

GLOSSARY

abolish (uh-BAH-lish) to permanently stop or end something

accomplice (uh-KAHM-pluhss) a person who uses their privilege to fight against supremacy

ally (AH-lye) a person who is aware of their privilege and supports oppressed communities

bubonic plague (byoo-BAH-nik PLAYG) a deadly sickness

deported (dih-PORT-ehd) having been kicked out or banished

Desi (DEH-see) a word that describes people from India, Pakistan, or Bangladesh

discrimination (dih-skrih-muh-NAY-shuhn) the unjust or unfair treatment of different categories of people

exotic (ig-ZAH-tik) special or foreign

exploiting (EK-sployt-ing) using in an abusive or selfish way

inclusive (ihn-KLOO-siv) allowing all kinds of people to belong

pandemic (pan-DEH-mik) a serious or deadly disease that spreads over multiple countries or continents

perpetual (puhr-PEH-chuh-wuhl) forever, never-ending

privilege (PRIV-lij) an unearned right or advantage given to a chosen person or group

quarantined (KWOR-uhn-teen-uhd) having been put or held in isolation to prevent the spread of disease

refugees (reh-fyoo-JEEZ) people who have been forced to leave their country in order to escape war, persecution, or natural disaster

scapegoat (SKAYP-goht) a person or group being blamed for wrongdoings, mistakes, or faults of others

stereotype (STEHR-ee-uh-type) a widely held idea or belief many people have about a thing or group, which may be untrue or only partly true

stigmas (STIG-muhz) marks of shame or disgrace

supremacy (suh-PREH-muh-see) the idea that one group is superior to other groups and thus is given privileges to maintain that power

xenophobia (zeh-nuh-FOH-bee-uh) the fear or dislike of people from other countries

INDEX